Table of Contents

Introduction

A crepe is a type of very thin pancake. Crêpes are usually of two types: sweet crêpes (crêpes sucrées) and savoury galettes (crêpes salées). Crêpes are served with a variety of fillings, from the simplest with only sugar to flambéed crêpes Suzette or elaborate savoury galettes. Crêpes originate in Brittany, a region in the west of France; the consumption is widespread in France, Belgium, the Netherlands, Canada, and many parts of Europe, North Africa, North America, Lebanon, Brazil and Argentina.

In France and Belgium, crêpes are traditionally served on Candlemas (La Chandeleur), February 2. This day was originally Virgin Mary's Blessing Day but became known in France as "Le Jour des Crêpes" (literally translated "The Day of the Crêpes", and sometimes called colloquially as "Avec Crêpe Day", "National Crêpe Day", or "day of the Crêpe"), referring to the tradition of offering crêpes. In fact, in 472 Pope Gelasius I offered Crêpes to French pilgrims that were visiting Rome for celebrating the Chandeleur. Also, the belief is that catching the crêpe with a frying pan after tossing it in the air with your right hand while holding a gold coin in your left hand would cause you to become rich that year. The roundness and golden color of a crêpe resemble the sun and its rays. This symbolism also applies to the coin held in the person's hand.

Types of crêpe

Sweet crêpes are generally made with wheat flour (farine de blé). When sweet, they can be eaten as part of breakfast or as a dessert. Common fillings include Nutella spread, preserves, sugar (granulated or powdered), maple syrup, golden syrup, lemon juice, whipped cream, fruit spreads, custard, and sliced soft fruits or confiture.

Savory crêpes are made with non-wheat flours such as buckwheat. A normal savory crêpe recipe includes using wheat flour but omitting the sugar. Batter made from buckwheat flour is gluten-free, which makes it possible for people who have a gluten allergy or intolerance to eat this type of crêpe. Common savoury fillings for crêpes served for lunch or dinner are cheese, ham, and eggs, ratatouille, mushrooms, artichoke (in certain regions), and various meat products.

Crêpes can also be made into crepe cakes. By adding the plain crepes on top of each other and within the two layers adds one layer of cream. It can also add anything you like, such as fruits, chocolate, cookies, marshmallow, and etcetera. Most of the crêpe cake is sweet and people usually consider it as a dessert. It can also replace the traditional birthday cake that people usually buy. Crêpe cakes are usually 15-30 layers, and the crêpes used are very thin and soft.

Batters can also consist of other simple ingredients such as butter, milk, water, eggs, flour, salt, and sugar.[8] Fillings are commonly added to the center of the crêpe and served with the edges partially folded over the center. An Indian variety of the crêpe uses a multi-grain flour called "bhajanee", eggs, curd, and an assortment of spices as its ingredients. It is a modern variation of an Indian dish called Thalipeeth.

In order to make an evenly thin crêpe, it is crucial to have a batter without lumps, which is difficult. After whisking the batter, it is best to let it rest for half an hour, or even overnight, to let the bubbles from whisking disappear from the batter. Some people even mix the batter to a fine consistency by using a blender or mixer. Also, a good machine will be a shortcut to making a better crêpe.

A crêperie may be a takeaway restaurant or stall, serving crêpes as a form of fast food or street food, or may be a more formal sit-down restaurant or café.

Crêperies are typical in France, especially in Brittany; however, crêperies can be found throughout France and in many other countries.

Because a crêpe may be served as either a main meal or a dessert, crêperies may be quite diverse in their selection and may offer other baked goods such as baguettes. They may also serve coffee, tea, buttermilk, and cider (a popular drink to accompany crêpes).

Special crêpes

Mille crêpes(ja) are a French cake made of many crêpe layers. The word mille means "a thousand", implying the many layers of crêpe. Another standard French and Belgian crêpe is the crêpe Suzette, a crêpe with lightly grated orange peel and liqueur (usually Grand Marnier), which is subsequently lit upon presentation.

English pancakes are similar to wheat flour crêpes and are served with golden syrup or lemon juice and sugar. Swedish pancakes, also called Nordic pancakes, are similar to French crêpes. In some of the Nordic countries, crêpes are served with jam or fruit, especially lingonberries (or the butter from that fruit) as a dessert with a variety of savory fillings. Traditional Swedish variations can be exotic. Besides the usual thin pancakes, called pannkakor in Swedish and räiskäle in Finnish which resemble the French crêpes and, often served with whipped cream and jam, are traditionally eaten for lunch on Thursdays with pea soup. The Swedish cuisine (as well as the Finnish one) has plättar/lettu, which resemble tiny English pancakes, are fried several at a time in a special pan. Others resemble German pancakes but are baked in the oven and include fried pork in the batter (fläskpannkaka). Potato pancakes called "raggmunk" contain shredded raw potato and may contain other vegetables (sometimes the pancake batter is omitted, producing rårakor).

A special Swedish pancake is the saffron pancake from Gotland which is made with saffron and rice and baked in the oven. It is common to add lemon juice to the sugar for extra taste. The pancakes are often served after a soup. Another special Swedish pancake is the äggakaka (eggcake), also called skånsk äggakaka (Scanian eggcake). It is almost like an ordinary Swedish pancake but it is much thicker and more difficult to make due to the risk of burning it. It is made in a frying pan and is about 1½ to 2 inches thick and is served with lingonberries and bacon. The Norwegian variety is commonly eaten for dinner, traditionally with bacon, jam (typically bilberry jam) or sugar.

The 49er flapjack is a sourdough crêpe which is popular in the United States, getting its name from the popularity of this style of pancake during the California Gold Rush. Because it is similar to a Swedish pancake, the 49er is sometimes served with lingonberry sauce, although most often it is rolled up with butter and powdered sugar, or served open-faced and topped with maple syrup.

Cherry Kijafa Crêpes are also common in the United States and are made with a traditional crêpe base, but filled with cherries simmered in a Kijafa wine sauce.

Crêpe dentelle is a crispy biscuit made with a very thin layer of crêpe folded in a cigar shape and then baked. It is usually enjoyed with a hot drink during the goûter, in France.

Overview: How to Make Crepes

Melt the butter: Melt some butter in the microwave or on the stove. Let it cool for a few minutes before using in the batter. (Otherwise you could scramble the eggs.)

Combine all ingredients in a blender: Add the cooled melted butter and all the remaining ingredients into a blender. A blender works WONDERFULLY to smooth out the batter because it cuts that flour perfectly into all the wet ingredients.

If you don't have a blender, just use a mixing bowl and whisk. I use my Ninja blender.

Chill the batter: Chill the crepe batter for at least 30-60 minutes before cooking it. This time in the refrigerator is crucial to the taste, texture, and success of your crepes. Use this time to clean up and get your skillet ready. You can even chill the batter overnight so it's ready to cook the next day.

Butter & heat a small skillet: Generously butter the pan and keep butter nearby for greasing the pan between each crepe too. Though professional chefs may use a specialty crepe pan, I find a small 8-inch skillet works perfectly at home. If you don't have a small skillet, use a larger one but make sure you keep the crepes THIN.

Cook crepes one at a time: The longest part of this recipe is standing over the stove and cooking them one at a time over medium heat. Use only 3-4 Tablespoons of batter per crepe. (I usually use 3 Tablespoons.) The less you use and the larger you stretch the crepe, the thinner they'll be. I twirl the pan so the batter stretches as far as it can go. If you don't do this, your crepes will be pretty thick and taste like tortillas. Still delicious, but very different. Flip the crepe over and cook the other side, too.

Serve with favorite fillings: I love serving them warm with cold whipped cream and fresh berries.

How to Make Crepes Ahead of Time
You can make the crepe batter up to 1 day in advance. Seal tightly in your blender or pour into a mixing bowl and cover tightly, then prepare crepes the next day. Crepes are best enjoyed right away, but you can make a batch and store in the refrigerator for up to 1-2 days. Reheat in the microwave or arrange on a lined baking sheet (they can overlap). Cover with aluminum foil and warm in a 275°F (135°C) degree oven for 10 minutes. You can also freeze crepes.

Key Ingredients

The recipe is written out below, but it's important you understand why each ingredient is used. This is a delicate batter, so substitutions aren't recommended.

Unsalted Butter: Butter is a key ingredient. Have extra butter handy for the skillet.

All-Purpose Flour: Flour is another key ingredient, providing the overall structure. I haven't tried any successful gluten free alternatives, but let me know if you do!

Granulated Sugar: These are lightly sweetened– you only need 1 Tablespoon.

Salt: A pinch of salt adds flavor.

Whole Milk & Water: Crepe batter needs liquid. Using all water created a limp and lacking crepe, while using all milk created a heavy crepe. For the best texture, use a mix of both. Trust me.

Eggs: As they do in pancake batter, eggs provide structure and bind all the ingredients together.

Vanilla Extract: Adds flavor– you'll definitely smell the vanilla as you cook these on the stove! Feel free to leave it out if you make savory style crepes.

Crepes Success Tips

Chill the batter: I mentioned this above and include it in the written recipe below, but it's definitely worth repeating. One secret to the BEST crepes is to chill the crepe batter for at least 30-60 minutes and up to 1 day. This time in the refrigerator enhances the batter's flavor and, more importantly, gives the flour a chance to fully hydrate.

Butter the pan between each crepe: The best part of crepes is the thin, delicate, and buttery crisp edges. To achieve this, butter the pan between EACH crepe. Sounds like a pain, but just grab a stick of butter and coat the pan before adding more batter. You won't regret it.

Twirl the pan: Pour the batter into the center of the hot and buttered pan. Lift the pan up and twirl it so the batter stretches as far out as it can go. (The thinner the crepe, the better texture it has– trust me.)

Crepe Fillings & Toppings

Crepes are a blank canvas for many different fillings and toppings. Though I'm all about going overboard with toppings like Nutella & bananas or apple pie filling & melted peanut butter, sometimes it's nice to keep things simple! Pictured is my favorite whipped cream flavored with fresh orange juice. Throw in a splash of orange liqueur if you have some lying around, too. Whip into medium peaks before filling or topping your crepes. I also serve these with tons of fresh berries. Lightly sweetened, the burst of fruit and citrus is a welcome refresher! With such a simple accompaniment, the crepes themselves truly shine.

Basic crepe recipe

ALLERGENS

Contains gluten , milk , egg , wheat and lactose.

INGREDIENTS

- 1 cup (150g) plain flour
- 1 teaspoon caster sugar
- 240ml milk
- 2 eggs

METHOD

Step 1

Place ingredients in a food processor or blender with a pinch of salt.

Step 2

Blend until smooth, then strain into a jug. Cover and set aside to rest for 30 minutes at room temperature.

Step 3

Dip a piece of paper towel in melted butter and use to brush base of a 16cm non-stick crepe pan or frypan over medium heat. When hot, pour in just enough batter to cover the base. Tilt pan so batter covers base in a thin film and pour any excess back into the jug. Cook crepe for about 1 minute until underside is golden, then use a metal spatula to flip. Cook other side for just under a minute until golden.

Step 4

Transfer to a plate and cover with foil to keep warm. Repeat for remaining crepe mixture, stacking crepes on the plate as you go.

RECIPE NOTES

To freeze cooked crepes, stack with greaseproof paper between each one. Wrap the stack in plastic wrap and freeze for up to 3 months. Defrost for 1 hour at room temperature.

Classic French Crepes
VARIETIES OF HOMEMADE FRENCH CREPES

Crepes come in two varieties –

Sweet crepes

Savory crepes

Sweet crepes are made with regular wheat flour (all purpose flour), and are usually slightly sweetened with sugar. These are perfect for breakfast or dessert. These sweet crepes are typically served with sugar, syrup, fruits, chocolate (or Nutella), whipped cream, or even ice cream.

Savory crepes are traditionally made with buckwheat flour. These are naturally gluten free, and have a nutty flavor because of the buckwheat flour. They are typically served for lunch or dinner, but they also work just as well for breakfast/brunch too. Savory crepes can be filled with savory fillings like ham, cheese, bacon, eggs, vegetables (like mushrooms), herbs and other types of meat filling too.

HOW TO MAKE PERFECT FRENCH CREPES

Homemade basic crepes are ridiculously easy to make, and difficult to mess up. The main ingredients for French crepes are flour, eggs and liquid (milk or water). According to Ruhlman, the ratio for these ingredients is 8 : 8: 4 (that is 8 oz of eggs or about 4 eggs, 8 fl oz of milk or 1 cup, and 4 oz of AP flour or scant 1 cup).

However, I find that this ratio gives me crepes that are a bit too eggy for my taste, so I add more milk and less eggs to my crepe batter.

WHAT IF YOUR CREPES BECOME RUBBERY?

There are two reasons for crepes turning out rubbery – too much gluten (flour), or cooking the crepes too slow. My French crepe recipe however eliminates these two problems.

With a liquid to flour ratio of 4:1 in this recipe, there's no risk of the gluten in the flour being overworked because of the increased amount of liquid present. Plus the resting time of 20

– 30 minutes for the batter also helps to keep the crepes soft.

If you're using a whisk, mix the flour with about half of the milk to create a smooth thick paste. Then add the rest of the liquid and mix it in, to make a smooth pancake batter.

However, I prefer using a stick blender, because I can add all the ingredients into a large bowl or a jug and just blend it all until everything is smooth (this only takes a few seconds). And for perfect results, I recommend leaving the crepe batter to rest for a little while to allow the gluten to rest.

The crepes are then cooked on a skillet over medium heat, allowing the crepes to be cooked in just over a minute. This quick cooking time allows your homemade crepes to be soft and buttery, without drying out.

FREQUENTLY ASKED QUESTIONS ABOUT MAKING CREPES

How can I make my crepes less rubbery?

With this recipe, your crepes will NOT be rubbery. With a liquid to flour ratio of 4:1, there's no risk of the gluten in the flour being overworked because of the increased amount of liquid present. Plus, the crepes are cooked over medium heat allowing them to cook quickly without drying out.

Can I make crepes gluten free?

Yes, you can make these gluten free. Buckwheat flour (gluten free) is also commonly used to make crepes in place of AP flour. But you can also use AP gluten free flour as well. The crepes will be more delicate, but will taste the same.

If you're looking to make crepes with almond flour, then I highly recommend looking for a KETO crepe recipe on google, that has been tested with almond flour.

Can I make these with self rising flour?

Yes, you can make these crepes with self rising flour, but keep in mind that the crepes will be thicker, because the baking powder in the flour will create lift in the crepes. While they won't be classic crepes, they will still be delicious!

Can I use whole wheat flour to make crepes?

If you prefer whole wheat flour over AP flour, you're welcome to make this substitution. But do note that the batter will taste nuttier and not as smooth as crepes made with AP flour. The finer the whole wheat flour, the better the homemade crepes will be.

Can I substitute the milk in this recipe?

Absolutely! You can use almond milk, cashew milk, soy milk, or any plant based milk to make these crepes. Some recipes even make crepes with just water, but I much prefer the added flavor of milk.

Can I make vegan crepes? Without eggs and milk?

Yes, this is possible. You can use a vegan egg replacement if you like. However, I prefer not to use flax seed egg because the crepe batter will have flecks of flax seed then.

I like to add some baking powder to my crepe batter that will make the batter lighter, and give it some strength as well.

HOW TO COOK PERFECT FRENCH CREPES

While there are fancy crepe pans in the market, you don't need an expensive crepe pan to make PERFECT basic crepes. A regular non stick skillet / pan works just as well. You can use just a French skillet pan to make the crepes as well, just make sure that the pan is buttered well so that the crepes don't stick. If you're new to making crepes, a regular non-stick pan is the best option.

Here I used a 10 inch pan to make 10 inch crepes. But you can just as well use an 8 inch or 12 inch pan as well, depending on what you have at hand.

8 inch pan – about 3 tbsp of batter (about 45 – 50 mL)

10 inch pan – about 1/4 cup of batter (about 60 mL)

12 inch pan – about 1/3 cup of batter (about 75 – 80 mL)

This is enough to create a thin layer of crepe batter on the bottom of each of these pans.

When the pan is hot, brush the surface with butter or oil. I prefer using butter.

Add the measured batter into the pan. Swirl the pan as you add the batter. Work quickly, to spread the batter evenly around the pan all way to the edges, so that you have a smooth edge. Continue to swirl the pan (and occasionally shake it gently), to move the batter around and fill the middle of the pan as evenly as possible.

Once the bottom of the pan is evenly coated with the batter, place it back on the heat and cook.

WAIT FOR BROWNING EDGES, BEFORE YOU FLIP OVER THE CREPE FOR CLASSIC FRENCH CREPES

this stage, you have TWO OPTIONS

For extra soft crepes:

Only cook the crepe until the surface of the crepe is set and there are no dry spots (only takes about 20 – 30 seconds). Then gently lift the crepe off of the pan (be careful as the crepe will be really soft), and flip it over for just a few seconds on the other side, if you like.

However when I make crepes like this, I don't cook the crepe on the second side at all.

This crepe will have very little browning (if at all).

For more traditional crepes:

Cook the crepes until the edges are starting to brown lightly, and they look a little crispy (about 40 – 50 seconds). Gently lift the crepe off of the pan, and flip it over for about 10 – 15 seconds on the second side, until you have caramelized brown spots.

This crepe will definitely have caramelization on both sides.

These are the kinds of crepes that are made at creperies and used in typical French crepe desserts.

When the crepes have been cooked, stack them up on a wire rack or plate.

When you're ready to serve/eat the crepes, simply cover them with another plate on top and microwave for about 30 seconds. The top plate allows the crepes to heat through steam, so that they don't dry out. Remove the top plate as soon as you're done microwaving so that the crepes don't become soggy. These basic crepes are best eaten warm.

The first crepe you cook is often the "tester", mostly because this is the best way to tell if the pan is properly heated and buttered well. So you can just make a smaller crepe first up, without wasting too much batter.

CLASSIC LEMON AND SUGAR CREPES

Crepes with lemon and sugar is a really classic way to serve French crepes. And it's easy too!

Simply sprinkle some sugar over one half of a warm crepe, then fold it into quarters. Top with lemon slices, some extra sugar and whipped cream, and serve! I prefer to use vanilla sugar over regular sugar, because the vanilla adds another subtle layer of flavor to this dessert. You can squeeze as much lemon juice over the crepes as you want and even dust them with powdered sugar if you like.

These lemon and sugar crepes are a delightfully sweet, tangy, refreshing and simple dessert! The salt also complements this dessert perfectly, and is also a reason why I don't like to sweeten my crepes too much.

Place one crepe on a plate

Step 2 for making lemon and sugar crepes - Sprinkle the sugar on one half of the crepe.

Sprinkle vanilla sugar over one half of the crepe

Step 3 of making lemon and sugar crepes - Fold over the crepe in half.

Fold over the crepe in half

Step 4 to make lemon and sugar vanilla crepes - Fold the crepe in half again. Serve with freshly squeezed lemon juice.

Fold over once more, and serve with fresh lemon juice

OTHER FILLING IDEAS

Sweet fillings for homemade crepes

My personal favorite – Nutella and banana

Strawberries (or any type of berry) and cream

Banana and caramel/butterscotch

Any fresh fruit with cream

Chocolate and strawberries

Lemon curd, or passion fruit curd and whipped cream

Ice cream, toasted nuts and chocolate sauce

Savory fillings for homemade crepes

Chicken and mushroom filling

Shrimp

Ham and cheese

Bacon and eggs

Ham and eggs

Omelette with herbs

Sauteed mushrooms

Curried meat filling to make Sri Lankan fried savory rolls (Chinese rolls)

HOW TO STORE EXTRA CREPES, OR MAKE THEM AHEAD OF TIME

I personally like to make the crepe batter the night before, and keep it covered in the fridge for next morning.

However, you can make the crepes ahead of time as well. Plus, if you make extra crepes, you can store leftover crepes for a later date too.

Classic French Crepes (Basic Crepes)

Ingredients:

Classic French Crepes

- 1 1/4 cup milk 10 fl oz
- 3 large eggs
- 2 tbsp oil or melted butter
- 2 tsp sugar for savory crepes, OR
- 2 – 3 tbsp sugar for sweet dessert crepes
- 1/2 tsp kosher salt
- 4 oz all purpose flour scant 1 cup

To Cook

- 1 – 2 tbsp softened butter
- Lemon and Sugar Crepes
- 1 – 2 lemons sliced thick or cut into wedges
- 1/4 cup vanilla sugar
- Whipped cream

Instructions:

1. Mixing with a Whisk

2. Place the milk and eggs in a jug/bowl. Whisk to combine (you should have about 2 cups of liquid).

3. Add the oil or butter and whisk it in.

4. Place the flour, salt and sugar in a large bowl.

5. Add about 3/4 – 1 cup of the liquid and mix gently to form a smooth paste. This should not take more than a few seconds. Take care not to over-mix.

6. Add the rest of the liquid and mix to form a smooth, watery batter.

7. Cover the batter and let it rest for at least 20 minutes. The batter can be kept in the fridge overnight as well.

Mixing with a Blender

8. Add the ingredients into the blender. Add the flour last. Blend for a few seconds until you have a smooth batter. You can use a stick blender as well for this purpose.

9. Cover the batter and let it rest for at least 20 minutes. The batter can be kept in the fridge overnight as well.

Cooking the Crepes

1. Preheat a 10 inch non-stick pan over medium heat.

2. Brush a layer of butter on the heated pan. I used a
    silicone brush, but you can use a butter soaked paper
    towel or cloth as well.

3. Always mix the batter first, before you make each
    crepe. This is to make sure the batter is uniformly
    mixed.

4. Pour 1/4 cup of the batter into the hot pan, and swirl to
    coat the bottom of the pan. Swirl and spread the batter
    along the edge of the pan first and then fill the middle
    with the remaining crepe batter. Make sure the batter
    is as evenly spread as possible.

5. Place the pan back on the heat to let the crepe cook.

6. For extra soft crepes – cook the crepes only until they
    are just set at the surface (about 30 seconds) and
    there's no browning on the edges. You can flip over
    the crepe gently, and cook for a few seconds on the

other side (optional), or remove the crepe from pan and place it on a plate.

7. For classic crepes – cook the crepes until the edges are starting to brown become a little crisp (about 40 seconds). Flip the crepes over and cook for a further 10 – 15 seconds on the other side until the crepes have caramelized spots.

8. Repeat until all the batter is used up (remember to mix the batter each time).

9. Stack the cooked crepes on a plate or wire rack.

Serving

If the crepes are no longer warm when you're ready to serve them, place another plate over your stack of crepes and microwave for about 30 seconds until the crepes are warm. Then remove the second plate quickly so that the crepes don't become soggy with steam/moisture.

Lemon and Sugar Crepes

1. Place a crepe on a plate or flat surface.

2. Sprinkle about 1 tsp of sugar over one half of the crepe and fold over in half. Then fold over one more time into quarters. Repeat with all the crepes.

3. Serve the French crepes with fresh lemon slices (that can be squeezed over the crepes before eating), and whipped cream.

Easy Crepe Recipe

INGREDIENTS

- 2 cups milk
- 4 eggs
- 3 Tablespoons butter , melted
- 1 Tablespoon sugar
- 1 teaspoon vanilla
- 1/2 teaspoon salt
- 1 1/2 cups flour , sifted

INSTRUCTIONS

1. In a blender, combine all of the ingredients and mix until batter is smooth (about 15-20 seconds). Refrigerate batter for at least 30 minutes, or overnight.

2. Spray non-stick cooking spray onto an 8-inch frying pan. Pour about 1/4 cup batter into the pan and cook over medium-low heat. Turn pan immediately from side to side to form an even circle. Cook for about 1-2 minutes per side, or until lightly browned. Remove from heat and stack until ready to serve.

3. Serve with your favorite toppings. Fresh fruit, jams, pudding, nutella, whipped topping and nuts are a few of our favorites.

NOTES

To keep warm: Place on a baking sheet in the oven at 175°F until ready to serve.

Leftovers: Add to a zip top bag and layer parchment or wax paper in between each crepe. Place in fridge until ready to enjoy.

To freeze: Store as directed above, then place in the freezer for about 1-2 months.

Reheating: Heat in microwave or skillet until warm.

Tiramisu Crepe Cake

This Tiramisu Crepe Cake Is:

Secretly simple

Creamy & light

Boozy, but you can skip the alcohol if desired

Best made ahead of time

Perfect if you're searching for a unique cake

Overview: How to Make Tiramisu Crepe Cake

Make the crepes. Crepe batter must chill for 30-60 minutes before cooking, then it usually takes about an hour to cook them all.

Make the tiramisu filling. You can do this ahead of time. More on the filling below.

Assemble the crepe cake. If you know how to spread creamy filling onto a crepe (like spreading butter on bread!), you can assemble a crepe cake. Using a fine mesh strainer, dust each layer of filling with cocoa powder. If you don't have one, skip the cocoa powder or use your fingers to sprinkle it on top.

If desired, pipe whipped cream on top.

Chill cake for at least 3 hours before slicing and serving. This time in the refrigerator helps the flavors develop and more importantly, allows the cake to set. If skipped, you won't be able to slice it.

The recipe below yields about 28 crepes. Use 25 in this cake. It's always convenient to have a few extra on hand if any crepes tear. Or let's be serious, if you want to taste test.

Crepes Success Tips

Chill the batter: I include this in the written recipe below, but it's definitely worth explaining. One secret to the best crepes is to chill the crepe batter for at least 30-60 minutes and up to 1 day. This time in the refrigerator enhances the batter's flavor and gives the flour a chance to fully hydrate.

Butter the pan between each crepe: The best part of crepes is their thin and delicately crisp edges. To achieve this, butter the pan between EACH crepe. Sounds like a pain, but just grab a stick of butter and coat the pan before adding more batter. You won't regret it.

Twirl the pan: Pour the batter into the center of the hot and buttered pan. Lift the pan up and twirl it so the batter stretches as far out as it can go. (The thinner the crepe, the better texture it has– trust me.)

Ingredients

- 6 Tablespoons (85g) unsalted butter, plus 5 more Tablespoons (70g) for the pan
- 2 cups (250g) all-purpose flour (spoon & leveled)
- 1/4 cup (50g) granulated sugar
- 1/4 teaspoon salt
- 2 cups (480ml) whole milk, at room temperature*
- 1/2 cup (120ml) room temperature water
- 4 large eggs, at room temperature
- 2 teaspoons pure vanilla extract

Tiramisu Filling

- 2 teaspoons espresso powder*
- 2 teaspoons warm water
- 1 and 1/2 cups (360ml) cold heavy cream

- 1 Tablespoon (15ml) rum or Grand Marnier* (optional)
- 8 ounces (1 cup) mascarpone, cold or at room temperature
- 1 cup (120g) confectioners' sugar
- 1 teaspoon pure vanilla extract
- 1/4 cup (22g) unsweetened natural or dutch-process cocoa powder (optional)

Whipped Cream Topping

- 1/2 cup (120ml) cold heavy cream
- 1 Tablespoon (15ml) rum or Grand Marnier* (optional)
- 2 Tablespoons (15g) confectioners' sugar
- 1 teaspoon unsweetened natural or dutch-process cocoa powder (optional)

Instructions

1. Make the crepes batter: Melt 6 Tablespoons of butter in the microwave or on the stove. Cool for about 5 minutes before using in the next step. The remaining butter is for the skillet.

2. Add the cooled melted butter, flour, sugar, salt, milk, water, eggs, and vanilla in a blender or large food processor. If you don't have a blender or food processor, use a large mixing bowl and whisk by hand. Blend on medium-high speed for 20-30 seconds until everything is combined. The mixture will be silky smooth and the consistency of cream, much thinner than pancake batter. Cover the blender tightly or pour into a medium bowl, cover tightly, and chill in the refrigerator for 1 hour and up to 1 day. This time in the refrigerator is imperative because it gives the flour a chance to become fully hydrated.

3. Cook the crepes: Use the remaining butter for greasing the pan between each crepe. Place an 8-inch skillet over medium heat and generously grease it with some of the reserved butter. If you don't have a skillet this size, use a larger one but make sure you keep the

crepes thin. Once the skillet is hot, pour 3-4 Tablespoons (closer to 3 is best) of batter into the center of the pan. Tilt/twirl the pan so the batter stretches as far as it will go. The thinner the crepe, the better the texture. Cook for 1-2 minutes, then flip as soon as the bottom is set. Don't wait too long to flip crepes or else they will taste rubbery. Cook the other side for 30 seconds until set. Transfer the cooked crepe to a large plate and repeat with the remaining batter, making sure to butter the pan between each crepe. If desired, separate each crepe with parchment paper so they do not stick together. Though, if using enough butter in your pan, the crepes won't stick. Yields about 28 crepes.

Loosely cover and set your crepes aside at room temperature as you prepare the tiramisu filling. You can also tightly cover and refrigerate the crepes for up to 1 day. Crepes must be room temperature or cold before you begin assembling the cake.

Make the tiramisu filling: First part of the tiramisu filling is to prepare concentrated espresso flavoring. Using a fork, mix the espresso powder and warm water together in a very small bowl. Set aside to cool down for a few minutes. You will mix it with the mascarpone. Using a hand mixer or a stand mixer fitted with a whisk attachment, whip the heavy cream and rum (if using) together on medium-high speed until medium peaks form, about 3-4 minutes. Medium peaks are between soft/loose peaks and stiff peaks. Set whipped cream aside. With a handheld or stand mixer fitted with a paddle or whisk attachment, beat the mascarpone, confectioners' sugar, vanilla extract, and cooled espresso liquid together on medium speed in a large bowl until combined and smooth, about 2 minutes. Fold the whipped cream into the mascarpone mixture. Don't worry if it looks curdled– mine sometimes does– it doesn't taste that way and will smooth out when it's stacked in the cake. Use filling immediately or cover and chill in the refrigerator for up to 1 day. Yields about 4 cups filling.

Assemble the cake: Spread 1-2 teaspoons of filling on the center of your cake stand or cake serving plate. This helps adhere the cake to the plate. Place a crepe on top. Spread about 2 heaping Tablespoons of filling evenly on top. If desired, dust with cocoa powder. Repeat layering crepes, filling, and a dusting of cocoa powder. Top with final and last crepe.

Whipped Cream Topping: You can frost the cake with whipped cream before or after chilling the cake in the refrigerator in step 9. My advice– I find it tastes better and slices easier if you chill the cake WITH the whipped cream on top. Using a hand mixer or a stand mixer fitted with a whisk attachment, whip the heavy cream, rum (if using), and confectioners' sugar together on medium-high speed until medium peaks form, about 3-4 minutes. Medium peaks are between soft/loose peaks and stiff peaks and are the perfect consistency for spreading or piping. Spread or pipe whipped cream on top of the cake. If you have extra, feel free to spread all around the sides of the cake too. If desired, dust with cocoa powder.

Refrigerate the cake for at least 3 hours and up to 1 day before serving. Chilling the cake in the refrigerator is imperative because the cake won't slice otherwise. No need to cover the cake if you're chilling it for only 3 hours. If chilling longer than that, I recommend loosely covering the cake.

Cover leftover cake and store in the refrigerator for up to 3 days.

Notes

Make Ahead & Freezing Instructions: Crepe batter, cooked crepes, filling, and assembled cake can all be prepared in advance. See the end of step 3, step 5, the end of step 6, and step 9. To freeze, prepare cake through step 8, but do not dust with cocoa powder on top. Tightly cover and freeze for up to 3 months. Remove from the freezer, evenly dust the top with cocoa, then thaw in the refrigerator for at least 24 hours. (Can thaw covered or uncovered.)

Milk: I prefer whole milk in the crepe batter. For a richer tasting crepe, half-and-half or heavy cream work too. 2% is

OK, but I wouldn't use lower fat milks. Any low fat or full fat nondairy milk works too.

Espresso Powder: You need very strong espresso for the filling. Here we are making it using espresso powder and water. If you can't find espresso powder, use instant coffee powder instead. You can also use 1 Tablespoon of super super super strong room temperature or cold black coffee instead of the espresso powder/water.

Alcohol: The filling and whipped cream topping include alcohol. I recommend rum or Grand Marnier. Skip the alcohol for a non-alcoholic version. No need to replace it with anything.

Cocoa Powder: Dusting cocoa powder between each layer, as well as on top of the crepe cake, is optional. If using, you can use natural or dutch-process cocoa.

Sweet and Savory Crepes

Ingredients

Sweet Crepes

- 1 Cup Flour
- 11/4 Cup Milk
- 2 Tbsp Butter
- 1/8 Tsp Salt
- 2 Eggs
- 2 tbsp Sugar
- 1 tsp Vanilla
- Savory Crepes
- 1 cup flour
- 11/4 Cup Milk
- 2 Tbsp Butter
- 1/8 Tsp Cayenne Pepper
- 2 Eggs

Instructions

1. Add all your ingredients together in a bowl and whisk
   it together until there is little to no lumps left in the

batter then pass the batter through a sieve and leave the batter to rest on the Tabletop for about 15 to 30 minutes or put it in the refrigerator for 1 hour and you can as well leave it

2. overnight in the fridge-This step is very important because it allows the gluten to rest so that you will not end up with a tough crepe.

3. Preheat a skillet or a heavy bottom non-stick pan (preferably between 9-12 inch pan), butter the pan and pour about 1/4 cup of batter into the pan, then tilt and rotate the pan to evenly spread the batter.

4. cook the first side is golden brown this should take about 1 to 2 minutes then flip to the other side and cook for a couple of seconds.

5. This savory version is best eaten hot while you can eat the sweet version hot or warm or at room temperature-the choice is yours!. Enjoy!!

Thin Breakfast Crepes

INGREDIENTS

- 1 cup (150 g) unbleached all-purpose flour

- 2 tbsp sugar

- 1 pinch salt

- 2 eggs

- 1 1/2 cups (375 ml) milk

- 1/2 tsp (2.5 ml) vanilla extract

- 1 tbsp unsalted butter, melted

- Softened butter, for cooking

PREPARATION

1. In a bowl, combine the flour, sugar and salt. Whisk in the eggs, ½ cup (125 ml) of milk and the vanilla until smooth. Gradually add the remaining milk, stirring constantly. Whisk in the melted butter.

2. Heat a 9-inch (23 cm) non-stick skillet over medium heat. When the skillet is hot, brush with a little softened butter.

3. For each crepe, pour about 3 tbsp (45 ml) of batter in the centre of the skillet. Tilt the skillet to spread the

batter evenly until it covers the bottom of the skillet. When the edge peels off easily and begins to brown, it's time to flip the crepe with a spatula. Continue cooking for 10 seconds, until cooked through, and remove from the skillet.

4. Place the cooked crepes on a plate as you go. Cover with aluminum foil to keep them from drying out and to keep them warm. Delicious with maple syrup or blueberry sauce.

Nutella Crepes

Ingredients

- 6 tablespoons unsalted butter
- 2 large eggs
- 1 large egg yolk
- 1/2 cup water
- 1 cup milk
- 1/2 teaspoon kosher salt
- 1 cup all-purpose flour

- 1/2 cup Nutella

Directions

1. In a medium nonstick pan over medium heat, melt the butter. Once the butter is melted, continue cooking until the butter is golden brown. Remove from the heat and set aside. The residual heat will make the butter a little more brown, so err on the side of golden brown versus dark before you turn off the heat.

2. In a medium bowl, gently whisk together the eggs, egg yolk, water, milk, and salt until just combined. Add the flour and whisk until smooth. Slowly pour the browned butter into the mixture, whisking constantly. If necessary, strain the mixture to remove any lumps.

3. Use a paper towel to wipe out the same nonstick pan used to melt the butter. Set the pan over medium heat. Using a 1/3-cup measure, scoop the batter and pour it into the center of the hot pan. Using a rotating motion with your wrist, swirl the

batter around and out to the edges of the pan- the thinner, the better. Return the pan to the heat and cook for 2 minutes. Use a rubber spatula to lift up the edge of the crepe and flip the crepe over. Cook on the other side for 30 seconds to 1 minute, depending on how golden you like it.

4. Slide the crepe onto a plate and spread with 1 tablespoon of the Nutella (or as much as you like). Fold the crepe in half, then fold in half again to form a triangle. You can also just roll up the crepe loosely like a carpet. Garnish with desired toppings.